THE Amazing INTERNATIONAL Space Station

by the Editors of YES Mag

Kids Can Press

To the kids who make it enjoyable (especially Vaughn, Leo and Casey) and to our editor, Val, who made it possible.

Acknowledgments:
Special thanks to: Simone Garneau, space consultant and cofounder of Futuraspace; Philip R. West at NASA, Johnson Space Center; Susan Lang at Cornell University

YES Mag is a bimonthly science magazine dedicated to introducing kids to science, technology and engineering in a fun and educational way.

The *YES Mag* team members who worked on this book are David Garrison, Shannon Hunt and Jude Isabella.

Kids Can Press acknowledges the financial support of the Ontario Arts Council, the Canada Council for the Arts and the Government of Canada, through the BPIDP, for our publishing activity.

Published in Canada by	Published in the U.S. by
Kids Can Press Ltd.	Kids Can Press Ltd.
29 Birch Avenue	2250 Military Road
Toronto, ON M4V 1E2	Tonawanda, NY 14150

www.kidscanpress.com

Edited by Valerie Wyatt
Designed by Julia Naimska

Printed and bound in Hong Kong, China, by Book Art Inc., Toronto

The hardcover edition of this book is smyth sewn casebound.
The paperback edition of this book is limp sewn with a drawn-on cover.

CM 03 0 9 8 7 6 5 4 3 2 1
CM PA 03 0 9 8 7 6 5 4 3 2

National Library of Canada Cataloguing in Publication Data

The amazing International Space Station / written by the editors of YES Mag ; illustrated by Rose Cowles.

Includes index.
ISBN 1-55337-380-4 (bound).   ISBN 1-55337-523-8 (pbk.)

1. International Space Station — Juvenile literature. I. Cowles, Rose, 1967– II. Title: Yes mag.

TL797.15.A49 2003   j629.44'2   C2003-900336-1

Contents

Space: Distant

Space — it's distant, dangerous and sometimes deadly. So why do we want to go there?

Space scientists and 'nauts (astronauts and cosmonauts) might answer that space exploration helps us better understand Earth, our solar system and the universe. It also encourages technological advances in fields from medicine to manufacturing. And orbiting satellites allow us to transmit phone and television signals around the world, or monitor the weather.

Anyone who has ever wondered why the sky is blue or what kind of butterfly will emerge from a chrysalis knows another answer — curiosity. Humans are naturally curious. We have a desire to understand and to know.

Space remains a mystery — we Earthlings have only been exploring it for about 50 years. But now we have a frontier outpost, the International Space Station (ISS), where 'nauts from different countries can live and work together.

and Deadly

'Nauts and scientists think of the International Space Station as the first stepping-stone to Mars. With a $100-billion price tag, the ISS is an expensive stepping-stone — but, hey, assembling a 450 t (tn.) laboratory in space was no easy task. It took 16 countries and more than 40 space missions to do it.

Can you see yourself as part of this far-out future? Maybe you'll be building the next space station or even trekking through the stars one day.

Either way you'll want to know how it all started, so pull up your space boots and put on your astronaut grin — we're off to the ISS.

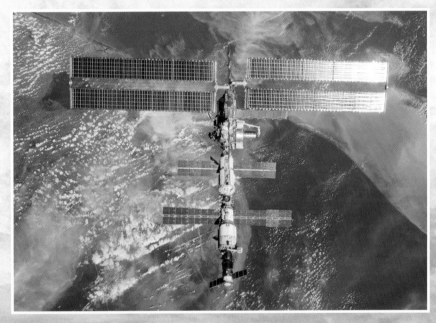

The International Space Station as of December 2001

The (Un)friendly Skies

Space is more than unfriendly to humans — it's downright hostile. But that didn't stop engineers, scientists and 'nauts from building the International Space Station. So what if there's no air, unbearable temperature extremes and deadly radiation — when you're constructing a space station, you have to be prepared to put up with hardships and danger.

Spacebound? Remember your spaceship. It's been specially designed to protect you from the hazards of space.

Wheeze!

At the top of Mount Everest, Earth's highest mountain, the air is so thin that humans have trouble breathing. But up where the ISS was built, there's nothing to breathe at all. Reminder to Earthlings: bring your own air supply.

Brrr & Whew!

Temperature extremes in space are enough to bake — or freeze — things, including human beings. Just how hot or cold it gets depends on several factors, such as the distance from the sun and the amount of sunlight absorbed. Up where the space station was built, 354 km (220 mi.) above Earth, objects, including human beings, could heat up to about 120°C (248°F) in direct sunlight and cool to about -155°C (-247°F) in darkness.

Ouch!

In 1983, a speck of paint about the size of the dot on this "i" smashed into a space shuttle window — and left a crater. More than 10 000 human-made objects, baseball-sized or larger, orbit Earth. Anything smaller than a large bolt, however, is not routinely tracked and can hit the station with the force of a hand grenade.

Zap!

In just one day, a 'naut in space is exposed to the same amount of cosmic radiation (energy traveling through space) as someone on the ground receives in a year. Solar flares erupting from the sun send out even more radiation, which can cause cancer, cataracts in the eyes and damage to the central nervous system.

Construction in the Cosmos

It took more than five years to build the International Space Station. The pieces — more than 100 — were first constructed on Earth, then ferried up into position by Russian and American spacecraft. Once in orbit, the 'nauts attached modules together like pieces of a huge LEGO set.

The first module left Earth in November 1998. It was the Russian-built Zarya Control Module. (Zarya means "sunrise.") A few weeks later, NASA launched the U.S.-built Unity Node and attached it to Zarya. The third major component was the Russian-built Zvezda Service Module. (Zvezda means "star.") About the size of a bus,

Zvezda was delivered and attached in July 2000.

The first ISS residents flipped on the lights in Zvezda in November 2000. Bill "Shep" Shepherd, Sergei Krikalev and Yuri Gidzenko — one astronaut and two cosmonauts — got along well, considering the cramped quarters. They spent a lot of time unloading and organizing supplies and waiting for the next delivery. That came one month later — huge solar arrays that gave the station more power and set the stage

for the U.S.-built Destiny laboratory module. This lab plays a key role in critical operations, such as life support, navigation, communications and research. It also gave the cramped first crew another room.

In April 2001, Canadarm2 was installed. This robotic arm was used to help construct the rest of the station. Canada was the third country to contribute a space station part. Others soon followed.

Japan built a four-piece lab named Kibo, meaning "hope" in

> "There is no hardware store around the corner, so if you forgot a particular type of washer or you don't have the right screwdriver, well, you can't go back and get it."
>
> — *Canadian astronaut Julie Payette*

Japanese. An outside platform for experiments in the harshness of space was Brazil's contribution. Italian scientists designed three Multi Purpose Logistics Modules — named Leonardo, Raffaello and Donatello after famous Italian artists (or maybe the Teenage Mutant Ninja Turtles). Like huge cupboards, they're sent up one at a time, attached to the space station and used until empty. Then they're shuttled back to Earth.

The European Space Agency (ESA) added the Columbus Orbital Facility, another laboratory for conducting research. The ESA also designed and built Automated Transfer Vehicles (ATVs). Each ATV docks with the ISS and delivers up to 9 t (tn.) of cargo, including fuel, food, clothes and even movies. On the way back down, the ATV incinerates as it hits Earth's atmosphere.

American astronaut Michael Lopez-Alegria uses a pistol-grip tool to put the finishing touches on the ISS. LEGO was never this complicated.

Pop Cans in Space

Some of the station's modules are just big pop cans — in shape and material. Think of them as cocoons, however. The shielding consists of an outer layer of aluminum in a waffle pattern for strength. Under this are layers of fibrous ceramic material and Kevlar — the stuff used in bulletproof vests — up to 10 cm (4 in.) thick around the aluminum shells of the modules. The windows each have four panes of glass that range from 1–2 cm ($\frac{1}{2}$–1 in.) thick. Outside, aluminum shutters provide extra protection when the windows are not in use.

Space Sims

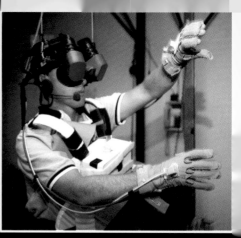

Training to build things in space doesn't actually happen in space. It's just too expensive. Instead, it happens right here on good old planet Earth in a series of space simulations. These "sims" are designed to look and feel like the real thing.

▲
▲
▲ **A computer gives a virtual reality simulation of constructing the space station — all inside this helmet.**

▲
▲
▲ **A roller-coaster flight in a special aircraft gives you a taste of what it's like to be weightless. It's no accident the plane's been nicknamed the Vomit Comet.**

Working in water simulates the microgravity of space. You feel weightless, yet cumbersome, just like you will when you're spacewalking.

Scouts never had it so hard. To prepare for their stay on the ISS, American astronaut Bill Shepherd (right) and Russian cosmonaut Sergei Krikalev attend a Russian survival training camp. In winter!

▶ ▶ ▶

No Sweat!

The view from the ISS is easy on the eyes, but constructing a space station is hard on the body. Moving the way you want to in space takes a lot of effort. And you can't wipe away the sweat streaming into your eyes — you're wearing a helmet.

Thick gloves make it hard to do small tasks and to hold onto the tools. Let something go and — oops! — it floats away to become dangerous space junk. And just to make things really interesting, every 45 minutes it's either sunrise or sunset — making it freezing or scorching. Are you having fun yet?

TRY A SPACE SIM

'Nauts wear thick heated gloves to protect their hands and keep them warm when working outside the space station. How easy is it to work with thick gloves? Try this simulation and see for yourself.

You'll need:

★ 3 pairs of gloves ★ paper clips ★ large cardboard grocery box (optional)
★ tape (optional) ★ scissors (optional)

1 Put on the 3 pairs of gloves. Try to pick up a paper clip in each hand and join them together.

2 For even more of a challenge, put 2 paper clips in a cardboard box, seal it with tape and cut two armholes. Now try to pick up the paper clips inside the box and join them together.

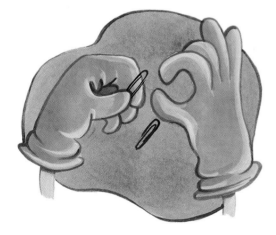

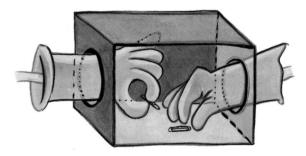

ISS Stats

Average operating altitude: 354 km (220 mi.)
Average speed: 28 000 km/h (17 500 m.p.h.)
Mass: 450 000 kg (1 000 000 lbs.)
Width: 108.5 m (356 ft.)
Length: 88.4 m (290 ft.)

Participating Nations

- Belgium
- Brazil
- Canada
- Denmark
- France
- Germany
- Italy
- Japan
- Netherlands
- Norway
- Russia
- Spain
- Sweden
- Switzerland
- United Kingdom
- United States

Introducing the ISS

The shuttle crew wave on their way to the launch pad. Leading the way in the front row are Pilot Stephen N. Frick (left) and Commander Michael J. Bloomfield (right); in the second row are Mission Specialists Rex J. Walheim and Ellen Ochoa; third row, Jerry L. Ross and Lee M.E. Morin; in the rear is Mission Specialist Steven L. Smith.

3-2-1 Lift Off!

So, you want to hitch a ride into space and see the ISS for yourself? Squirm into your flight suit — hope orange is your color — and step into your waiting taxi, the space shuttle *Endeavour*.

You belt yourself in and hear voices. Aliens? No. It's NASA's Mission Control Center (MCC) contacting you. You answer, "We are go for a launch at T minus five seconds and counting … Five, four, three, two, one …" You're off!

While MCC radios you about how great the launch was, you're pinned against an uncomfortable metal seat, feeling like a gorilla is parked on your chest. Hey, what can you expect when you're in the nose of a rocket blasting into space. Despite the bone-jangling, teeth-rattling experience (and the gorilla), you're all smiles.

Two things shoot you so far so fast: the Solid Rocket Booster (SRB) engines and the shuttle's main engines, supplied with liquid fuel from the External Tank (ET).

The SRBs take the shuttle up 44.8 km (28 mi.). Two minutes after launch, you're cruising at 4950 km/h (3075 m.p.h.) and the SRBs separate, parachuting down and landing somewhere in the Atlantic Ocean for pickup and re-use on later missions. A few minutes later, Main Engine Cut Off (MECO) occurs. The now-empty External Tank is chucked and mostly burns up in the atmosphere.

Once in space, the shuttle uses its Orbital Maneuvering System (OMS) to boost itself up to the minimum orbiting altitude, 249 km (155 mi.) above Earth. Total travel time: eight minutes. Now the chase is on. It takes you a mere 41 hours to find your orbiting "parking spot" — the International Space Station. Finally, it's in your sights, and you're ready for docking.

Which button gets the space shuttle to warp speed?

Dock here.

Space Parking

About 33.5 m (110 ft.) from the space station, you flip on the Reaction Control System (RCS). Then you start to maneuver in closer. It's a bit like playing a video game. You grasp the Rotational Hand Controller (RHC), which looks suspiciously like a joystick. You're too low and need to raise the nose, so you tilt back on the controller.

The movement fires rockets in the nose downward to rotate the nose up.

A mere 9 m (30 ft.) away, the shuttle stops. For the next five minutes or so, you fine-tune the shuttle's position to line it up with the large, black cross on the station's docking port. Finally, you ease the shuttle in and a series of hooks engage. You've made it! But wait a minute — or 120 minutes, to be exact. That's how long it takes for the passageway between the shuttle and the ISS to fill with air, allowing you to enter the space station.

"*Endeavour* arriving!" you announce as you float through the hatch. Welcome to the ISS.

Ship's Log: Dec. 2, 2000
"We get a visual on Endeavour in trail, about 5–8 km (3–8 mi.) out in a very bright light. Approach smooth … View looking down on the orbiter is very unreal — more like a model than 100-ton object — you just can't put a sense of scale to it … Felt and heard a very slight bump as contact was called … Rest of the docking sequence felt very smooth … [Afterward] we float around the wardroom looking for some more food, talking about the docking and what we will find in the Node tomorrow."

The space shuttle *Endeavour*

POPPIN' ROCKETS

You can build your own rocket out of a film canister and watch it blast sky-high.

You'll need:

★ a Fuji brand film canister and lid (many photo labs give empty canisters away for free)
★ baking soda ★ vinegar ★ safety goggles

Note: Do this project outside. The baking soda and vinegar reaction makes a mess! Plus your rocket is going to fly high! As soon as you put the lid on the film canister, move out of the way and stand well back.

1 Remove the top of the film canister and pack the lid tightly with baking soda.

2 Fill a quarter of the film canister with vinegar.

3 Put on your safety goggles. Then gently put the lid on the film canister and snap it closed.

4 Turn the canister upside down, put it on the ground and quickly stand back. After a few seconds, the canister will blast off. If your rocket fizzles, try a film canister with a tighter-fitting lid.

What's Happening?

You are creating a chemical reaction. The vinegar reacts with the baking soda and produces carbon dioxide gas. The gas builds up until the small canister can no longer contain it and the canister separates from the lid, shooting sky-high.

When Up Is Up — and Down

What could be more fun than floating through the hatch to your home away from home, the ISS?

That floating feeling is a result of microgravity. What is microgravity? Here on Earth, Earth's gravity pulls us, and everything else, toward the center of the planet — and keeps us from floating around. The space station is also being pulled toward Earth by gravity. Because

Three crews just hanging around the space station — Expedition Two (red shirts), Expedition Three (white shirts) and the shuttle crew (striped shirts).

the crew and the space station are falling at the same rate, 'nauts experience weightlessness, or microgravity.

Sounds like fun — until you discover that *everything* is affected by microgravity. Try putting a pen down. It floats away. Try sitting. Sorry, you float away.

No gravity means the 'nauts vertebrae spread apart, making them taller and forcing their muscles to stretch. The good news? 'Nauts grow about 2–5 cm (1–2 in.). The bad news?

American astronaut Susan Helms and Russian cosmonaut Yury Usachev aboard the Destiny lab.

Ah, space — where the air is your lounge chair! American astronaut Michael Bloomfield free floats.

What Goes Up ...

Imagine riding in an elevator car to the top of a very, very tall building. At the top, the cables supporting the car break, causing the car and you to fall. Since you and the elevator car are falling together, at the same rate, you would feel as if you were floating. You would be experiencing "free fall," another term for microgravity. It's fun. Until you, um, hit the bottom.

Backaches. To relieve the pain, 'nauts often float around in a fetal position.

Then there's the pesky sinus problem. Fluids in a 'naut's body, normally held down by gravity, rush toward the head. That's why 'nauts look puffy in photos taken soon after launch. Rumor has it they also feel like they're standing on their heads.

Weightlessness has more serious concerns. With all that liquid going up, the hydration sensor located in the upper body thinks there's plenty of water sloshing around. This means you don't feel thirsty, so dehydration can be a problem — at least until your body adjusts.

A longer term problem of living in microgravity is bone loss. Without the resistance that occurs when we fight gravity, muscle and bone waste away. To deal with this, 'nauts spend time in the gym — up to two hours a day.

Sounds like a lot of work — and worry — for the fun of floating. Is it worth it? Ask a 'naut and the answer is, "You bet!"

... Must Come Down

Gravity pulls the ISS toward Earth. Why doesn't it get pulled all the way down? The ISS orbits at roughly 28 000 km/h (17 500 m.p.h.) — just the right speed to balance between flying off into space and falling down to Earth. Eventually, however, gravity wins, as the ISS is slowed by atmospheric drag and drifts too close to Earth. So the station's propulsion thrusters were designed to boost it back up where it can keep the right balance of speed, for a while at least.

Life on the ISS

model of ISS

cutlery

jam

honey

floating fruit

B arfing, sneezing and sore backs eventually take a backseat to coping with everyday life on the ISS — the simple acts of eating and sleeping become adventures. Come on board and join the crew for a visit and a not-so-quick bite to eat. Most days, the ISS 'nauts have 90 minutes to prepare and eat a meal. Here's how food prep happens.

You go to the Zvezda Service Module, where the galley is located, and grab a meal tray. You choose a meal listed on the computer. (The meals are selected five months before liftoff. 'Nauts must decide then what they want to eat for their entire stay on the ISS.) Menus have been analyzed for nutritional content. One nutrient of concern during long stints in space is

American astronaut James Voss juggles his snack — didn't his parents tell him not to play with food?

vitamin D, which is important for bone health. The lack of ultraviolet light, due to spacecraft shielding, limits the ability of 'nauts to produce this vitamin naturally.

But back to the computer. You type in "chicken teriyaki with

'Nauts share a meal while American astronaut Scott Horowitz acts as their floating waiter.

Former American astronaut Mike Mullane once built a floating solar system using a blob of orange juice as the sun and M&Ms as the planets.

stir-fried vegetables." The computer tells you which drawer to find your meal in. You put the packaged meal into a convection oven. While the chicken and veggies are heating, you rehydrate some wonton soup by plugging in a needle-shaped water faucet and pressing the hot water button. To stop fluid from escaping, you slurp the soup through a straw that has a clip at the end.

When the chicken and veggies are cooked, you take the package out of the oven and Velcro it to the tray. Then you strap the tray to a table and start to eat. Take it slowly — no sudden movements. Knocking over your meal would mean floating chicken and veggies.

Small squeeze bottles — sort of like eye-drop bottles — containing salt water and pepper water let you season your food.

For dessert, there's a fortune cookie. Your fortune: You have the ability to rise above others.

Cookies for breakfast? Nutritious crumb-free cookies, called Russkoye or Vostok, are a staple for Russian cosmonauts. The cookies even appear on the morning menu for the station's crew.

Give that man a crazy straw! American astronaut Brian Duffy tests a space drink at NASA's Johnson Space Center. From the look on his face, it's hard to tell if he likes it.

Flying Food

Food is delivered to the ISS by the space shuttle or the Russian Progress supply vehicles about once a month. A delivery means fresh fruits and veggies. Most food is made to last — it's dehydrated, frozen or processed, and packaged in pouches and cans. The packaging is ultra important. It must withstand pressures rarely exerted by your average grocery store clerk: the cans experience the same jarring forces the 'nauts feel during takeoff.

Space food must also be germ free — no one wants sick astronauts. On Earth, the acceptable amount of bacteria for canned food is about 300 000 bacteria per g (8 500 000 per oz.). In space, it's a minuscule 8 bacteria per g (225 per oz.). Food must also be solid — sauce floating around is not only messy, it's germ friendly.

Runaway cans! Where's the Velcro when you need it?

'Nauts join in a toast by "clinking" bags of juice.

Cosmonauts delivered pizza to Yury Usachev, commander of the second ISS crew. The topping was salami. Pepperoni failed the food safety test.

Space Soup

One day in the future, 'nauts may grow their own food in space. Cornell University researchers are cooking up mostly vegetarian recipes from ingredients that can be grown hydroponically (in a nutrient-rich liquid) in artificially lit, temperature-controlled space habitats. This carrot soup, created by Rupert Spies, could be made from ingredients grown in space and might eventually find its way to a 'naut's dinner table. Ask an adult to help you whip up a batch.

You'll need:

- ★ 750 g (1 $\frac{1}{4}$ lbs.) sliced carrots
- ★ 250 mL (1 c.) diced onions
- ★ 15 mL (1 tbsp.) cooking oil
- ★ 1L (4 c.) soy milk (unsweetened)
- ★ 250 mL (1 c.) vegetable broth or water

- ★ 2 mL ($\frac{1}{2}$ tsp.) each of ground ginger and nutmeg
- ★ salt and pepper
- ★ 45 mL (3 tbsp.) fresh, chopped parsley

1 In a medium saucepan, sauté carrots and onions in oil for two minutes.

2 Add the soy milk, broth, ginger, nutmeg, salt and pepper. Heat through but do not boil. Simmer until the carrots are tender.

3 Ask an adult to help you pour the soup into a food processor and purée for a few seconds.

4 Return the soup to the pan and add half the parsley. Serve the soup and garnish with the remaining parsley.

What's Happening?

Space food must be tasty, nutritious, economical, easy to prepare and use few ingredients. (Cargo weight is at a premium.) It must also be low in salt. Why? In space, urine is cleaned and recycled into water. Too much sodium (salt) in water used to irrigate crops would harm the growing plants.

Clean Up!

Russian cosmonaut Mikhail Tyurin gives American astronaut Frank Culbertson a haircut. (Frank sucks up clippings with a modified vacuum.)

There are no fights over dirty dishes on the International Space Station — everything is chucked into the trash compactor. But there is other cleaning to do, and for that there's nothing like good old-fashioned elbow grease. The ISS crew keeps surfaces clean by — are you ready for this? — wiping them down with a mild soap.

All surfaces are cleaned about every two weeks, more often when food is spilled. Not only do 'nauts make a mess, they are the mess. 'Nauts lose up to 3 g (.11 oz.) of skin daily. This dead skin, lint, plus all the other stuff that makes up dust, free floats around in the station. The debris eventually finds its way to air filters, which also pick up tiny hitchhikers called microorganisms.

'Nauts bring microorganisms — fungi and bacteria — with them into space and liberally sprinkle them around the station. People-eating aliens from interstellar space pale in comparison to what these renegade life-forms could do. With no natural competitors in space, colonies of microorganisms could choke out any other life.

Air filters get rid of the dust and microorganisms, then the filters are vacuumed to keep

Canadian astronaut Chris Hadfield does the windows.

Breathe Easy

Imagine sharing a cramped space for months without showers or even a window that opens. Whew!

Relax — you can breathe easy on the ISS. It's equipped with machines that scrub the air and provide fresh oxygen. While some oxygen is stored, most comes from water electrolysis, a process that uses electricity from the station's solar panels to split water molecules into hydrogen and oxygen.

Great! Now you've got oxygen to breathe in, but what about the carbon dioxide you breathe out? Some of it is vented into space. The rest is combined with the hydrogen to produce water and methane. The water is re-used, and the methane is released into space.

them clean. But one other hitchhiker, mold, is immune to all that vacuuming and filtering. Mold, a fungi, especially loves humidity and will eat just about anything. Fungus was actually eating through the glass portholes of the Russian space station *Mir*. To discourage mold,

the ISS is kept dry. Its humidity levels are set at 65 to 70 percent. Unfortunately, that means more flaky skin — and more cleaning!

Ship's Log: Dec. 11, 2000 "*Went thru the ship with the vacuum cleaner — pulled all the debris out of filters and intakes. It is amazing — if you ever let [go] of something, there is an almost 100 percent chance it is going to end up in a filter or screen somewhere.*"

Plastic bags help control the mess when the food starts to fly.

Shape Up 'N

auts need to keep fit, not to keep that pizza from going straight to their thighs, but to combat muscle and bone loss. On Earth, we strength-train every day just by fighting gravity. But in space, microgravity does nothing to keep you from losing bone and muscle fast. No gravity, no resistance!

The longer you stay in space, the more bone you lose. Scientists estimate that on a nine-month mission to Mars, up to 45 percent of a person's bone mass could be lost. While muscles are relatively easy to rebuild once on Earth again, bone is a different story.

So head for the treadmill, a Teflon-coated aluminum sheet on a roller, that locks onto the floor. Strap yourself in and start walking. Don't forget to exercise your arms by pushing upward on the attached bar. Air blowing from a nearby duct will dry off perspiration. Otherwise, sweat would stick to your skin and grow thicker and thicker.

Bored with the treadmill? For variety, buff up on a rowing machine or an exercise bicycle called the velo-ergometer. Remember to put everything away; the mini gym shares the service module, Zvezda, with the galley, a couple of sleeping compartments and work and communication stations. And you don't want to block the view through one of the 13 windows. Or get in the way when the Russian *Soyuz* spacecraft is docking.

American astronaut James Voss cycles to nowhere in the Zvezda Service Module.

All work and no play makes for bored 'nauts. So what do 'nauts do for entertainment? Canadian astronaut Marc Garneau loves baroque music, so he brought along a CD. He also packed CDs of Canadian jazz musicians Diana Krall and Oscar Peterson. Russian cosmonaut Yuri Gidzenko brought the Beatles, Rolling Stones and a collection of Russian folk songs.

Music is popular with 'nauts, and each has a Discman. Other space pastimes? E-mailing friends and family and watching movies on DVD. Space-shuttle missions deliver new DVDs, but it can take a while, and 'nauts have been reduced to watching flicks such as the History of Navy SEALS to while away some downtime. They never tire, however, of one leisure activity — Earth-gazing. Looking out the window is so popular, the windows get smudged!

American astronaut Ellen Ochoa watches as the world turns.

Expedition Two and shuttle crew go Hawaiian.

Ship's Log: Jan. 5, 2001 "Finished the 2nd disk of 2010. Something strange about watching a movie about a space expedition when you're actually on a space expedition."

Good Night

You've worked for at least eight hours. Exercised for two. Spent a lot of time preparing your meals. Contacted friends and family by e-mail. Watched a Russian movie with subtitles, and now you're pretty tired.

On the ISS, 'nauts store their personal stuff, look for quiet time and sleep all in a "bedroom" smaller than your average bunk bed. But at least they have somewhere quiet to go. Actually, it's not all that quiet. The rattle of fans and machinery force the crew to wear earplugs when they sleep.

When it's time to catch some zzzzs, 'nauts pull off their slipper-socks and outer clothing, storing everything in a net. They climb into their sleeping bags and pull up the long zipper on the front of the bag, then snap together straps around their waists to hold them securely in their bunks. One warning: in the microgravity of the space station, arms float out in

Russian cosmonaut Yury Usachev jots down some notes in his cozy sleeping compartment in the Zvezda Service Module. See the photo of his family?

front like Frankenstein's monster's. To keep that from happening, 'nauts slip their hands through loops on the side of the sleeping bag.

Sleep is scheduled for eight hours, but often 'nauts wake frequently, especially during longer space missions. Scientists believe that in space the body's internal clock is disrupted. This clock regulates the body's daily production of melatonin, a sleep-promoting hormone, and cortisol, a hormone that promotes wakefulness. The clock is reset every day by the rising and setting sun. But on the station, one "day" is just 90 minutes long — bright half the time, dark the other half. So while some 'nauts take sleeping pills, on average, 'nauts still sleep two hours less each night than on Earth.

Ship's Log: Nov. 24, 2000 "Noise is a distraction, but bearable. We are getting reasonable sleep, all hands wearing earplugs."

American astronaut James Voss shaves. Let's hope he brushes his teeth too — check out the candy bars on the wall.

Good Morning

You wake up and struggle out of your sleeping bag. Time to head for the little closet with the toilet. You place your feet under a pair of straps, sit down on the small seat and clamp the restraints over your thighs. Now fire up the fan that acts like a vacuum cleaner under your bum. Zoom! The solid waste gets sucked into a holding tank. Urine goes into a separate tank — on the ISS it's recycled into oxygen and water.

Shaving is done with a razor, electric or manual. Toothbrushing is not much different than on Earth, except that you use an edible toothpaste or "spit" into a towel. A rinseless shampoo helps keep your hair and scalp clean, and a sponge bath takes care of the rest of you. Water, however, is a good place for micro menaces to flourish. To keep the water safe, a catalytic oxidator heats water to 130°C (266°F).

So who cleans the bathroom? Everyone. The toilet is wiped down after each use.

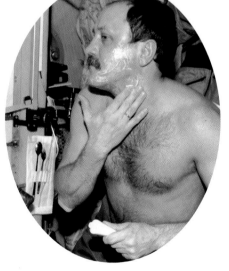

Do 'nauts get a closer shave in space? Cosmonaut Yury Usachev shaves with a regular razor blade and shaving cream on the International Space Station.

Astro Ambling

Uh-oh! Those big solar arrays need some maintenance — time for you to head outside for a spacewalk, or EVA (extravehicular activity) in space talk. While an EVA is exceedingly dangerous, it's the most spectacular part of station life.

So there you are, hanging out over Earth, with only a few layers of space-age materials separating you from the universe (and certain death). At least you have the latest accessory in space fashion — heated gloves. Oh, and by the way, you're loving it!

Step One

Getting ready for an EVA means going into the air lock and slapping on a big diaper — you can't just whip back inside for a bathroom break.

Step Two

After that comes the Liquid Cooling and Ventilation Garment, a mesh suit made of nylon and spandex **A**. Tubes of water run through it to keep you cool.

Step Three

The Electrical Harness is next **B**. It has wires that allow communication with the ISS and Mission Control. Vital signs are also monitored. (Mission Control gets concerned if your heart stops beating.) Slip on the "Snoopy Cap" with headphones and microphones **C**.

Step Four

Now you struggle into the suit. First, you climb into the Lower Torso Assembly (LTA): the pants, knee and ankle joints, boots and lower waist **D**. Now shimmy into the Hard Upper Torso (HUT), and connect it by a metal ring to the LTA. Arms, gloves and helmet are attached the same way **E**.

Step Five

An Extravehicular Visor Assembly (another EVA) slips over your helmet **F**. It consists of a gold-covered, sun-filtering visor, a clear thermal-impact protective visor, and adjustable blinders. Four small headlamps help you see what you're doing.

Step Six

The Portable Life Support System (PLSS) **G** — oxygen tanks, carbon dioxide scrubbers, cooling water, radio, electrical power, ventilating fans and warning systems — is indispensable. With the PLSS, you can cruise space for nine hours. If the PLSS fails, a backup sits just below it. The Secondary Oxygen Pack (SOP) gives you 30 minutes to get back inside.

Step Seven

Mount the Display and Control Module (DCM) **H** on your chest. It's used to operate the PLSS with help from the mirror **I** attached to your arm. You also have a checklist attached to your arm to help you remember things while out on a seven-hour spacewalk.

How long did it all take? A mere 45 minutes to get out of the air lock, with about 113 kg (250 lbs.) of gear to lug around.

A 'naut and a suit are like an independent spacecraft. Cost? Twelve million dollars for the suit. The rest is, of course, priceless.

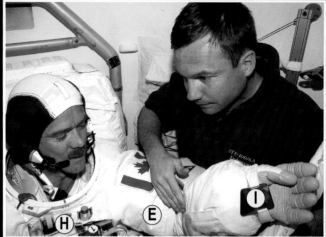

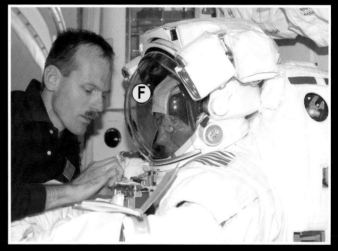

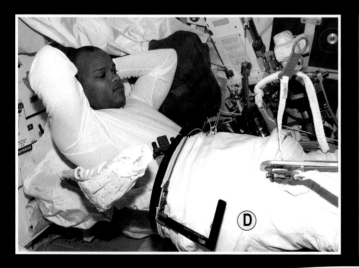

"It doesn't pay to fight the suit.
The suit will win, so you have to learn
how to be one with the suit."

— American astronaut Jim Newman

Space Science

Space offers something unique to scientists — an environment with little gravity. So 'nauts not only run the space station, they also follow instructions from ground-based scientists on how to conduct certain experiments in this unique environment.

'Nauts grow protein crystals for cancer research and monitor their own reflexes, among other "experiments." Probably the most useful knowledge, however, will come from research on how the human body responds to long-term exposure to microgravity. If we're going to keep on exploring space, some crucial questions must be answered.

Here is a sampling of the experiments that have been conducted so far on the space station.

Experiment #1: Protein Power

Proteins are building blocks of life. To learn more about proteins, scientists need protein crystals — the bigger and more perfectly formed the better. The crystals tend to grow bigger in space without the tug of Earth's gravity. Bigger protein crystals are easier to study, so 'nauts have been growing crystals in space since 1985.

Scientists send up experiments with new techniques for growing crystals, and the 'nauts try them out. One day, crystals grown in space may help scientists on Earth learn more about crystal shapes and develop drugs for diseases, such as cancer and diabetes. Research on zeolite crystals may even make for changes to the way gasoline is processed here on Earth.

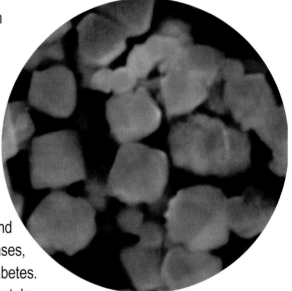

Crystals grown on Earth (top) are smaller than ones grown in space (bottom).

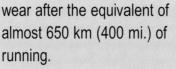

Spacey Spin-offs

Sneakers and space technology have more in common than you might think. In 1990, an athletic shoe manufacturer used space technology to create a new sneaker mid-sole, which showed no visible signs of wear after the equivalent of almost 650 km (400 mi.) of running.

Over the years, space technology has found its way into everyday life here on Earth. These secondary uses of space technology, called spin-offs, include an advanced pacemaker and wheelchair, infrared thermometer, computer reader for the blind, retail store bar codes, quartz timing crystals, household smoke detectors, radiation-blocking eyeglasses, self-righting life raft, portable computer, heart rate monitor, scratch-resistant sunglasses coating and cordless products.

CRYSTAL GROWING FOR EARTHLINGS

Using salt, you can grow crystals right here on Earth — although they won't be perfectly formed like the ones the 'nauts grow in microgravity. Make sure you look at the shape of the Epsom salts crystals before you add them to the water. Use a magnifying glass so you can see them clearly. After your crystals grow, look at *their* shape.

You'll need:

★ 125 mL ($\frac{1}{2}$ c.) water ★ 50 mL ($\frac{1}{4}$ c.) Epsom salts (bath crystals)
★ a shallow container or dish ★ a sponge (optional)

1 Get an adult's help to carefully boil the water in a pot. Remove the pot from the heat and add Epsom salts. Stir until dissolved.

2 Pour the mixture into a shallow container. There should be just enough to cover the bottom. (You can pour the mixture over a sponge if you want. It will make the crystals a bit easier to see, because they will form around the sponge.)

3 Put the container in a safe, sunny place. As the water evaporates, crystals will start to form.

What's Happening?

You boil the water because salts dissolve in hot water better than in cold water. As the solution evaporates, salt crystals are left behind on the sponge or in the container. What shape are the salt crystals you grew?

Experiment #2: Plant Power

Plant experiments are an important part of space station science. There's even an Advanced Astroculture plant growth chamber — a totally enclosed, automated "greenhouse" — for finding out what plants do in space.

The ISS 'nauts have grown batches of a weed known as thale cress. A comparison with similar plants on Earth helps scientists understand how plant life cycles are affected by microgravity. That information is important to the future of space exploration — plants will be used for food and even to clean

and replenish air and water supplies. Long stays in space will require generations of plants that grow reliably.

Russian cosmonaut Yury Usachev looks happy with the Astroculture plant experiment.

Experiment #3: Shock Power

In 2001, three members of the ISS crew got "zapped" as part of an experiment that tested human endurance on long space voyages.

In the experiment, a mild electrical shock was applied to the backs of their knees. The response — called the Hoffman Reflex — allowed researchers to measure calf muscle contractions. And *that* told them how well the spinal cord responds to stimuli. If spinal-cord response decreases during a long space flight, it may be that exercise programs are

less effective the longer 'nauts are in space. Exercise programs would have to be redesigned.

American astronaut Frank Culbertson "runs" on Zvezda. Electrical zaps to 'nauts' muscles can tell scientists if exercise really helps.

Ship's Log: Jan. 5, 2001 "Shep and Sergei set up the JASON plant growth experiment in the Node. The plant samples, which are to be light-exposed, are now decorating the quarter-deck. We were checking the seed types in the hope one might be 'palm tree'."

Whatever you do, hold on tight! American astronaut Patrick Forrester collects data on how materials weather in space.

Experiment #4:
Phantom Power

Radiation in space is a problem for 'nauts. In 2000, a solar storm pounded the station with so much radiation that it forced the first crew to take shelter in the heavily shielded aft (back) end of the Zvezda Service Module for 12 hours.

To estimate the amount of radiation on body organs, especially blood-forming organs, 'nauts conducted the Phantom Torso experiment. The torso is a "phantom" because it is not human, but closely mimics human tissues and organs. In fact, the torso is so human the 'nauts have named it Fred. Radiation measurements on Fred were recorded by the crew and transmitted to scientists on Earth every 10 days.

That's no dummy — that's Fred, the Phantom Torso.

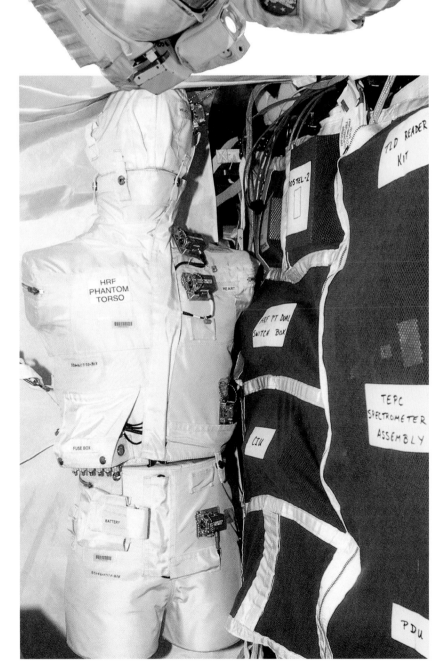

D-A-N-G-E-R!!!

No matter how prepared you are, things can still go wrong. And in space that can spell D-A-N-G-E-R! What if your tether (safety line) snaps while you're on a spacewalk? You might find yourself free floating toward Mars. Good thing you're wearing your handy-dandy SAFER (Simplified Aid for EVA Rescue) pack.

You grab the SAFER joystick. It controls 24 small jets that fire pressurized nitrogen gas and lets you maneuver around. Cruising speed is 2 km/h (1 m.p.h.). Top speed? Only 11 km/h (7 m.p.h.). Slow but steady. Oh, by the way, you have enough fuel for only 13 minutes.

Okay, it's just not your week. On your way back to the space station — zing — a micrometeoroid slices a hole in your spacesuit. Don't worry. Your suit has an emergency "blowdown" oxygen supply that can be tapped to keep it inflated for 30 minutes, even with a 20 cm (8 in.) hole. That should be enough time to get back on board. You hope.

Suppose something big hits the space station itself? A small crew (three or fewer) could use the *Soyuz* as an escape vehicle.

The X-38 "lifeboat"

But when the ISS has a full crew of seven, 'nauts will use a yet-to-be-built, seven-person "lifeboat" called the X-38. This agile spaceship has been designed so it can be undocked in less than three minutes and make an emergency landing back on Earth in just three hours. If necessary, the entire descent can be made without help from Mission Control.

When the X-38 reaches an altitude of 7000 m

The X-38 is suspended under a giant parafoil during a test flight.

(23 000 ft.) above Earth, the 'nauts will slowly unfurl the X-38's huge parafoil. Although the X-38 is designed to land automatically, a backup system will allow the crew to steer it.

"If you didn't have that tether and you let go, even if you're two inches away from the station, you can't swim over there. There's no water to create forces against."
— *American astronaut Mike Gernhardt*

First Crew

The station's first crew, Expedition One, blasted off from Russia on October 31, 2000. For four months, the three 'nauts shared a space the size of a bus. Eating, sleeping and working together, this team pretty much wrote the manual for the crews that followed. Who are these guys?

Expedition One: Crew Commander

William "Shep" Shepherd
Born: July 26, 1949
Hometown: Babylon, New York
Hobbies: Sailing, swimming, working in his garage
Education: Bachelor of science in aerospace engineering, U.S. Naval Academy, 1971. Degrees in ocean and mechanical engineering from Massachusetts Institute of Technology, 1978.

The sea is in Shep's family. His dad was a U.S. Navy pilot who went on to work in the aerospace industry. Shep wanted to be a pilot like his dad, but failed the eye exam. Instead, he became a Navy SEAL and an underwater demolition expert. He joined NASA in 1984.

Shep is a handyman. He likes to tinker in his garage, so he brought tools with him to the ISS. It's a good thing he did, because the crew needed them — they had a lot of improvising to do. He's also a softie. For the holidays, Shep brought up Christmas stockings for his two crewmates.

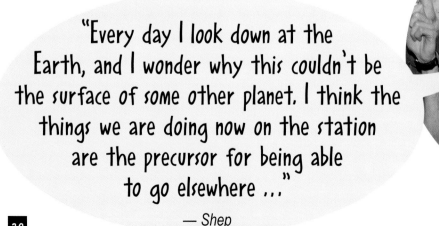

"Every day I look down at the Earth, and I wonder why this couldn't be the surface of some other planet. I think the things we are doing now on the station are the precursor for being able to go elsewhere ..."

— *Shep*

Expedition One: Crew Flight Engineer

Sergei Konstantinovich Krikalev

Born: August 27, 1958
Hometown: St. Petersburg, Russia
Hobbies: Swimming, skiing, cycling, aerobatic flying, amateur radio operations
Education: Mechanical engineering degree, St. Petersburg Technical University, 1981.

Sergei has spent nearly 16 months in space since becoming a cosmonaut in 1985, most of it on the space station *Mir*. His bosses thought he was so good, they volunteered him as a member of the first ISS crew.

> "Traveling outside of Earth I remember this feeling of being part of mankind."
> — *Sergei*

He was in space at the time! When he returned home, Sergei found out about his new job while watching the TV news. That was in 1996.

As a boy, Sergei wanted to be a pilot and cosmonaut. As a young man, he was part of the national aerobatic flying team, placing first in the Soviet Union in 1986. He's also a dedicated ham (amateur) radio operator and used a radio aboard the ISS to talk to other ham fans and schoolchildren.

Expedition One: Crew Pilot

Yuri Pavlovich Gidzenko

Born: March 26, 1962
Hometown: Elanets, Russia
Hobbies: Team sports, swimming, tennis, football
Education: Graduated from Kharkov Military Aviation College of Pilots, 1983. Graduated from Moscow State University in land surveying and cartography, 1994.

Young Yuri wanted to be a military pilot like his father. He realized his dream after graduating from college. Then officials at the Gagarin Space Training Center suggested Yuri take the exam to be a cosmonaut. He went into space as commander of a *Mir* mission for six months in 1995–96. He was training for another *Mir* mission when his bosses suggested — or ordered — that he switch to the ISS. He was glad he did, even though he had to sleep in a corner of the Zvezda Service Module. At least he got a new sleeping bag when space shuttle *Endeavour* visited.

> "This provides new horizons, new knowledge."
> — *Yuri*

"You can see the atmosphere — a thin, multicolored veil on the rim of the horizon — and entire weather systems. You can be working outside and be distracted by Africa going by. You go from white, blinding sun into absolute pitch darkness in about 15 seconds."

— Canadian astronaut Chris Hadfield

Big Blue Marble

Highways, cities and fields of crops — you can see them all from the ISS. Earth-gazing is a popular pastime for 'nauts. They bring books with them, but often they end up just looking at Earth. As cosmonaut Sergei Krikalev said before blasting off, "You can read when you're back here on the ground."

Hey Earth! Say Cheese

The ISS 'nauts spend 10 to 20 minutes a day taking photographs of Earth. The space shuttle delivers film and picks it up for developing. Their photographs provide a record of the changes to Earth's surface, particularly to coral reefs, smog-prone urban regions, and areas experiencing major floods or droughts triggered by El Niño. The ISS shutterbugs also photograph high-altitude glaciers, faults along tectonic plate boundaries, and unusual features, such as meteor impact craters.

Changes in photographs taken over three decades give scientists a good idea of impacts — both human and natural — on Earth.

Window on the World

The ISS has the biggest window ever designed for a spacecraft — 50 cm (20 in.) across. Developed by Dr. Karen Scott (below), it's also the highest quality optical window ever installed in a crewed spacecraft. Scott's window consists of a thin exterior "debris" pane, primary and secondary pressure panes and an interior "scratch" pane.

So You Want to Be an Astronaut

"**A**stronaut" comes from Greek and means star sailor. "Cosmonaut," also from Greek, means sailor of the universe.

Americans and Russians have traditionally dominated the ranks of 'nauts because their countries have put a lot of effort into space programs. But with the 16-member partnership of the International Space Station, lots of other nations are heading into space.

It's Never Too Early to Start

Sounds like a cliché, but it's true. Work on the basics, especially science and math. In high school, get good grades. University is a must —

engineering, biology, chemistry, geology, physics and math are common 'naut choices. Astronauts must have at least a bachelor of science degree and three years of related experience. Most hold masters' or doctoral degrees, too.

Hitting the books is important, but so are other types of training, such as flying planes, parachute jumping and scuba diving.

Application to the Stars

Check out your country's space program on the Web to see what their requirements are. But beware: the competition is stiff. For example, NASA has accepted applications every two years in the past. Out of an average of 4014 applicants, only 20 are chosen.

★ Out of 195 former and present astronauts, 123 were involved with scouting as kids. That's 64 percent!

★ To be a pilot astronaut, you must be no shorter than 1.6 m (5 ft. 4 in.) and no taller than 1.9 m (6 ft. 4 in.). As a mission specialist, you can be as short as 1.5 m (5 ft.).

★ While English is the official language on the ISS, Russian is definitely important. The station's first crew said they spoke in "Runglish," a mixture of English and Russian.

★ Want to be rich in Russia? Don't be a cosmonaut. Their salary amounts to $3000 a year.

SPACED OUT

This simple experiment gives you a little taste of what it's like to be a 'naut.

You'll need:

★ an office chair (the kind you can spin around)

1 Sit on the chair.

2 Now imagine that you are floating in the space station. Can you turn yourself around to reach something just behind you without touching the floor or walls?

3 Try to turn yourself all the way around.

What's Happening?

If you think turning yourself around is an awful lot of work, think about how hard it is for 'nauts. In space they have little control over their movement — just like you in the chair.

The Race to Space

circa A.D. 160	Greek satirist Lucian of Samosata writes a story of a trip to the moon. The moon dwellers eat frogs, sweat milk and sport beards down to their knees.
1232	The Chinese use "arrows of flying fire" to drive back attacking Mongols. It will be some time before rockets are used as anything other than weapons.
1500	Chinese scientist Wan Hu builds a flying machine out of 47 gunpowder rockets strapped to the back of a chair. Unfortunately, he doesn't survive the test flight. 
1687	English mathematician Isaac Newton publishes a book describing gravity and three laws about forces and how things move. The thrust of a rocket is an example of Newton's third law of motion: "To every action, there is an equal and opposite reaction."
1783	The Montgolfier brothers launch a balloon carrying a sheep, a duck and a rooster. After eight minutes, the balloon lands safely. The animals are fine and the first to really fly. 
1865	French novelist Jules Verne writes a story in which his characters travel to the moon in a craft fired by a huge cannon. His book is so convincing that hundreds of readers believe the spaceship exists and volunteer to go along on the first trip.
1903	Konstantin Tsiolkovsky, a self-educated Russian scientist, sketches spaceships fueled with liquid oxygen and liquid hydrogen. Often known as the "father of astronautics," Tsiolkovsky also proposes multistage rockets and describes spinning habitats in which people can live under artificial gravity—space stations. The tombstone on his grave reads "Mankind will not remain tied to Earth forever."

| 1926 | At his Aunt Effie's farm in Massachusetts, American physicist Robert Goddard launches the first-ever liquid-fuel-propelled rocket. It rises to a height of 12.5 m (41 ft.), reaching a top speed of 100 km/h (62 m.p.h.). |

1942 As World War II rages, a team led by German engineer Wernher von Braun successfully launches a liquid-propellant rocket called the V-2 (or "Vengeance Weapon 2"). Soon, V-2s carrying warheads full of explosives are bombarding Britain and other countries. After the war, von Braun designs space rockets for the U.S., including the *Saturn V* rocket, which later puts humans on the moon.

1957 In October, the space age really gets underway with the Soviet Union's launch of *Sputnik I*, the world's first artificial satellite.

1957 In November, the Soviets launch *Sputnik 2*, which carries a dog named Laika. She is the first Earth creature in space and proves that life can survive there. Unfortunately, her air supply runs out after a week, and she does not survive the trip.

1959 The Soviets launch a spherical spacecraft called *Luna 2*. It is the first spacecraft to land on the moon.

1961 Soviet jet pilot Yuri Gagarin is the first human in space. After circling Earth once, his capsule re-enters Earth's atmosphere. Gagarin safely ejects and parachutes to the ground.

1963 A Soviet factory worker and amateur parachutist named Valentina Tereshkova becomes the first woman in space.

1967   Despite the decade's successes, space flight is certainly not without its dangers. *Soyuz 1* crashes on its return to Earth, killing Soviet cosmonaut Vladimir Komarov.

1969   "Houston, Tranquility Base here. The Eagle has landed." With these words, Lunar Module *Eagle*, carrying American astronauts Neil Armstrong and Buzz Aldrin, touches down on the moon.

1970   In an effort to gather more information about the body's response to prolonged microgravity, two Soviet cosmonauts spend 18 days in space aboard *Soyuz 9*.

1971   *Salyut 1* is the first of many large structures sent into orbit by the Soviet Union. Designed for long periods of human habitation, it's the first true space station.

1981   Space shuttle *Columbia* is safely launched and returned to Earth. It lifts off like a regular rocket but can be used on other missions because it returns to Earth like a plane.

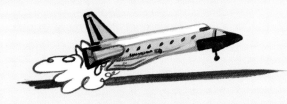

1986   The Soviets launch the first components for a space station. Called *Mir* ("world" or "peace" in English), the station survives dangerous fires and a near fatal collision to remain in space three times longer than planned. In 2001, after more than 86 000 orbits of Earth, *Mir* makes its final fiery plunge into the South Pacific.

1986   Just 73 seconds after liftoff, the space shuttle *Challenger* explodes, killing all seven crew. The terrible accident is caused by a faulty O-ring seal between segments on one of the solid-fuel booster rockets.

1994   Russian cosmonaut Dr. Valery Polyakov sets a record for the longest time in space. He returns to Earth after spending 438 days aboard the *Mir* space station.

1998   The first component of the International Space Station is launched. More than 40 launches will be required to complete the station.

2003   Tragically *Columbia* and her crew of seven are lost on re-entry in February.

The Secret Language of Space

"Is there a BIT for this BLIM on the CAL to CASE? The SMART are reading some ELF. With our HEDS we give our FEAT to the OATS, and with MAGIK we shouldn't need to use any PEP. We would need a COSMIC COP for our HAB's FAB if you ever finish that SQUID PIE."

Hey, if you're going to become a 'naut and get involved in HEDS, you've got to know the lingo. Use the list below to translate the terms above and in the rest of this book.

ATV	Automated Transfer Vehicle
BIT	Built-In-Test
BLIM	Berthing Latch Interface Mechanism
CAL	Common Air Lock
CASE	Crew Accommodations and Support Equipment
COP	Co-Orbiting Platform
COSMIC	Computer Software Management and Information Center
DCM	Display and Control Module
ELF	Extremely Low Frequencies
EMU	Extravehicular Mobility Unit
ESA	European Space Agency
ET	External Tank
EVA	Extravehicular Activity or Extravehicular Visor Assembly
FAB	Flight Assignment Baseline
FEAT	Final Engineering Acceptance Test
HAB	Habitation Module
HEDS	Human Exploration and Development of Space
HUT	Hard Upper Torso
ISS	International Space Station
LTA	Lower Torso Assembly
MAGIK	Manipulator Analysis, Graphics and Integrated Kinematics
MCC	Mission Control Center (Houston)
MECO	Main Engine Cut Off
OATS	Optical Alignment Transfer System
OME	Orbital Maneuvering System
PEP	Portable Emergency Provisions
PIE	Particle Impact Experiment
PLSS	Portable Life Support System
PMA	Pressurized Mating Adapter
RCS	Reaction Control System
RHC	Rotational Hand Controller
RMS	Remote Manipulator System
SAFER	Simplified Aid for EVA Rescue
SM	Service Module
SMART	Safety and Mission Assurance Review Team
SRB	Solid Rocket Booster
SOP	Secondary Oxygen Pack
SQUID	Standard Quick Release Universal Interface Device

Index